Fact Finders®

IMMIGRATION
★ TODAY

IMMIGRANTS

FROM

AFGHANISTAN

AND

THE MIDDLE EAST

BY NEL YOMTOV

CONSULTANT:
KARYN D. MCKINNEY, PHD
ASSOCIATE PROFESSOR
OF SOCIOLOGY
PENN STATE ALTOONA

CAPSTONE PRESS
a capstone imprint

Fact Finders Books are published by Capstone Press,

1710 Roe Crest Drive, North Mankato, Minnesota 56003

www.mycapstone.com

Cataloging-in-publication information is on file with the Library of Congress.

Names: Yomtov, Nelson, author.

Title: Immigrants from Afghanistan and the Middle East / by Nel Yomtov.

Description: North Mankato, Minnesota: Capstone Press, 2019. |

Series: Fact Finders: Immigration Today | Audience: 8–10.

Identifiers: LCCN 2018005318 (print) | LCCN 2018011490 (ebook) | ISBN 9781543513844 (library binding) | ISBN 9781543513882 (paperback)| ISBN 9781543514001 (eBook PDF) |

Subjects: LCSH: Middle Easterners—United States—Juvenile literature. | Afghans—United States—Juvenile literature. | Immigrants—United States—Juvenile literature. | Middle East—Emigration and immigration—Juvenile literature. | Afghanistan—Emigration and immigration—Juvenile literature. | United States—Emigration and immigration—Juvenile literature.

Classification: LCC E184.M52 (ebook) | LCC E184.M52 Y66 2019 (print) | DDC 973/.0494—dc23

LC record available at https://lccn.loc.gov/2018005318

Editorial Credits

Editor: Jennifer Huston

Production Artist: Kazuko Collins

Designer: Russell Griesmer

Media Researcher: Eric Gohl

Production specialist: Laura Manthe

Source Notes:

p. 18: http://www.bbc.com/news/magazine-38885611

pp. 26, 29: http://www.sacbee.com/news/investigations/afghan-refugees/article84313357.html

p. 28: http://www.sacbee.com/news/investigations/afghan-refugees/article85856422.html

Printed in the United States of America.
PA021

TABLE OF CONTENTS

CHAPTER 1

Where Is the Middle East?

4

CHAPTER 2

The Big Move

10

CHAPTER 3

A New Life

20

CHAPTER 4

What's Next?

26

Glossary 30

Read More 31

Internet Sites 31

Critical Thinking Questions 31

Index 32

★

WHERE IS THE MIDDLE EAST?

Imagine being forced to flee your homeland to settle in a different country. You leave behind everything important to you—family members, friends, and school. You may not even know the language spoken in your new country. How would you feel? Many **immigrants** face these challenges in countries all over the world.

The first group of immigrants from the Middle East arrived in the United States during the late 1800s. They came from several countries. The region known as the Middle East doesn't have any formal boundaries. But most people agree that it is made up of approximately 20 countries.

The Middle East features a wide variety of ethnic groups, languages, and religions. Arabs comprise the largest ethnic group in the region. Kurds, Persians, and Turks also make up a large part of the region's population. Arabic is the most widely spoken language, followed by Persian (also called Farsi), Turkish, Kurdish, and Hebrew.

The Middle East is home to Islam, Christianity, Judaism, and many other religions. Most people living in the region are Muslim, meaning that they follow the religion of Islam.

MIDDLE EAST

MOROCCO

TUNISIA

MEDITERRANEAN SEA

CYPRUS

TURKEY

AFGHANISTAN

LEBANON

SYRIA

IRAN

ISRAEL

IRAQ

KUWAIT

PALESTINE

WEST BANK

BAHRAIN

PAKISTAN

JORDAN

UNITED ARAB
EMIRATES

ALGERIA

LIBYA

EGYPT

RED SEA

SAUDI
ARABIA

QATAR

OMAN

YEMEN

INDIAN OCEAN

immigrant—someone who comes from one country to live permanently in another country

★ COMING TO AMERICA ★

People from Afghanistan and the Middle East move to the United States for various reasons. Some go to escape **persecution** based on their religion or race. Christians made up the earliest wave of immigrants from the Middle East to the United States. In the 1880s they fled what are now Syria, Lebanon, and Iraq to escape **discrimination** from Muslim rulers. Like the Pilgrims—the first European immigrants to America—these Christians from the Middle East simply wanted to practice their religion.

People also leave their homeland to escape poverty or to find better jobs. Many parents decide to leave so their children can receive a better education. People living in poor nations often move for better health care too.

A BOOMING COMMUNITY

In the early 20th century, many Middle Eastern immigrants came to work in the automobile industry in Detroit, Michigan. Thousands of others started small businesses, such as grocery stores and gas stations. Today this area in southeastern Michigan has the largest population of Arab Americans in the United States. In fact, it has one of the largest Arab communities outside the Middle East. Many of the Arab Americans in this area are Muslims from Lebanon, Iraq, and Yemen. Iraqi Christians also make up a large part of the area's Middle Eastern population.

Many immigrants go to the United States to be with family members who already live there. Immigrants already living in America offer a support system to new arrivals. Arab and non-Arab immigrants from the Middle East often live and work with family members who have previously immigrated.

After arriving in the United States, immigrants are often greeted by family members already living there.

persecution—cruel or unfair treatment, often because of race or religious beliefs
discrimination—treating people unfairly because of their race, country of birth, or gender

★ A CHOICE . . . OR NOT? ★

Some people choose to leave their homeland and settle in the United States for safety reasons. Each year thousands of **refugees** leave their home countries. Some leave to escape the impact of natural disasters, such as earthquakes, hurricanes, and floods. Others leave because of poverty in their home countries.

Many refugees from Syria escaped to Turkey and Greece in boats.

 refugee—a person forced to flee his or her home country because of war, poverty, natural disaster, or persecution

Some refugees flee to escape war and violence. In 2011 a civil war erupted in Syria. Because of the danger, more than 11 million people were forced to leave the country in the years after the fighting began. By 2017 about 18,000 Syrian refugees had moved to the United States.

Children stand in front of a destroyed home before their family flees war-torn Syria.

WAVES OF NEWCOMERS

The United States has experienced four main waves of immigration. During the 1600s and 1700s, British immigrants arrived to establish settlements on the East Coast. From about 1815 to 1865, most immigrants came from western Europe, especially Ireland and Germany. From 1880 to 1920, people from central, eastern, and southern Europe came by the millions during a third wave of immigration. During that time, Italians as well as Jews from Russia, Romania, and Austria-Hungary were among the largest number of immigrants. During the fourth wave, which took place after 1965, most immigrants came from Mexico, Central America, and Asia.

CHAPTER 2

THE BIG MOVE

Moving to America can sometimes be a long and costly process. Just ask Munther Alaskry and his family.

In 2003 during the Iraq War (2003–2011), Munther met a group of U.S. Marines. Munther was a student at the University of Technology in Baghdad, Iraq. After hearing how well he spoke English, the soldiers offered him a job as a **translator**. Over time Munther held a series of jobs translating for U.S. military units. He also helped train Iraqi troops. He even worked with a unit that cleared bombs planted by the enemy terrorist group al-Qaeda.

Because he worked for the Americans, members of al-Qaeda threatened to kill him. He fled to Jordan for a brief time, but he went back to Iraq after a few years. In 2008 Munther married his wife, Hiba. In 2009 their daughter, Dima, was born. Munther now had a family to care for, and he knew that staying in Iraq placed them in grave danger.

 translator—someone who changes written or spoken material from one language into another

Munther Alaskry risked his life working with U.S. Marines during the Iraq War.

To hide from al-Qaeda, the Alaskry family moved frequently. In 2010 Munther decided to move his family to the United States. But first he had to apply for a special immigrant **visa** (SIV). SIVs were granted to people who worked with the U.S. military in Iraq. When U.S. troops began leaving Iraq the following year, Munther was on his own. Without the protection of the American soldiers, Munther and his family desperately needed the visas.

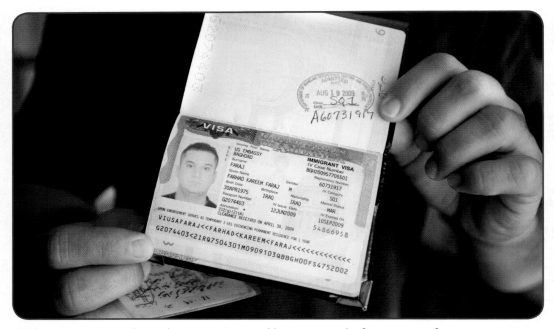

Without a visa, such as the one pictured here, people from many foreign countries are not allowed to enter the United States.

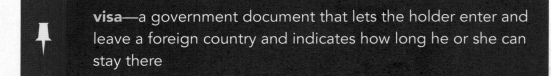

visa—a government document that lets the holder enter and leave a foreign country and indicates how long he or she can stay there

The Special Immigrant Visa (SIV) Program

In 2007 the U.S. government began granting SIVs for Iraqi and Afghani translators who worked for the U.S. military. Since then, more than 70,000 people have moved to the United States because of the SIV program.

Since 2013 the number of Afghanis coming to America on the SIV has been on the rise. At the same time, the number of Iraqis going to the United States on the SIV has declined. This shift is because the U.S. military now has a smaller presence in Iraq than Afghanistan. In previous years, the opposite was true. The number of SIVs allowed depends on the size of the U.S. military presence. However, each country is also only permitted a certain number of SIVs. Since 2014 applications for SIVs from Iraq are no longer being taken.

After long delays and applications, the Alaskry family received their visas in December 2016. After waiting nearly seven years, they were finally able to move to the United States. Munther bought airline tickets for their journey, which was scheduled for January 28, 2017. Their trip would begin with a short stop in Istanbul, Turkey. Their final destination was Houston, Texas, where friends were waiting.

★ A TROUBLED BEGINNING ★

In the early morning hours of January 28, Munther watched American news programs from his home in Iraq. He saw President Donald Trump sign an **executive order** banning immigration from Iraq and six other Muslim countries for 120 days. It was Trump's first important executive decision since taking office a week earlier. The order was designed to keep terrorists out of the United States. Iraq was included on the list because the terrorist group ISIS is active there.

The news troubled Munther, but he still had a plane to catch with his family. Later that morning the Alaskrys and their two young children boarded an airplane in Baghdad. Three hours later the plane landed in Istanbul, and the family transferred to a plane bound for Houston. The Alaskrys were happy and excited to finally be heading to the United States.

But before the plane took off, a police officer approached the Alaskrys in their seats. After checking their **passports**, the officer removed the family from the plane. News of President Trump's order had reached Turkey. The Alaskrys spent the next 13 hours sleeping in chairs at the Istanbul airport. They were sent back to Iraq the next morning.

President Trump signs an executive order that kept people from several Muslim countries from entering the United States.

executive order—an order that comes from the U.S. president or a government agency and must be obeyed like a law

passport—an official booklet that proves a person is a citizen of a certain country; passports allow people to travel to foreign countries

The Alaskrys' dream of starting a new life in America was crushed. Saddened and discouraged, the family returned to their house in Iraq and began thinking about their next move. But before they left for America, they had sold their car and their furniture, and Munther had quit his job. The apartment that was waiting for them in Houston was given to another family.

Worse, the Alaskrys' visas were going to **expire** in two months. If that happened, nearly seven years of waiting would have been for nothing. They would have to start the entire application process over again.

 SUCCESS

Just a few days after being removed from the plane, the Alaskry family received good news. Americans protesting President Trump's order had convinced lawmakers to change the policy. Certain visa holders—such as the Alaskrys—were again permitted to enter the United States.

 expire—to reach the end of the time when something can be legally or properly used

People from all over the world were angry with Trump's travel ban.
The protest shown here took place in London, England.

In early February the Alaskrys once again headed to the Baghdad airport. But this time the family was not as cheerful or hopeful. They knew anything could still go wrong. The Alaskrys boarded a plane to Qatar, the first stop on their journey to America. This time everything went smoothly, and the family landed safely in New York City.

After landing, the Alaskrys were taken to a room and interviewed by airport officials. For five hours Munther and Hiba answered the officials' questions.

The Alaskrys were finally in America, where they would make their new home in Rochester, New York. Over the years, Rochester has welcomed hundreds of refugees from Iraq and other countries. The Alaskry family's long, anxious wait to live in America was finally over.

"Now they are in the best country in the world . . . ," Munther said of his children. "This is my dream, to bring my kids here."

A group called No One Left Behind helped the Alaskry family get settled in the United States. U.S. soldiers founded the group to help former Iraqi translators start over in the United States. No One Left Behind arranges for special immigration visas and helps the new arrivals find jobs and homes.

The Alaskry family arrived at John F. Kennedy International Airport in New York City on February 3, 2017.

A NEW LIFE

Yalda Kabiri was one of the few female translators employed by the U.S. military during the War in Afghanistan (2001–present). Yalda was in the fourth grade in Kabul when the Taliban terrorist group banned girls from attending school. In 2001 U.S. troops pushed the Taliban out of Kabul. After that, Yalda returned to school and began learning English.

After high school Yalda became a translator in a medical unit at a U.S. air base. But Yalda kept her job a secret. She feared the Taliban would harm her if they found out she worked for the Americans. One time an anti-American taxi driver tried to kidnap Yalda and her daughter. But they jumped out of the car and fled to safety.

Not willing to take any further risks, Yalda applied for a special immigrant visa. In 2013, while pregnant with her second child, she received the visa. But her husband Zabihullah's request for a visa was denied.

Yalda Kabiri worked as a translator helping U.S. troops in Afghanistan.

Nevertheless, Yalda bought airplane tickets to America for herself and her daughter Sana. An agency that aids immigrants helped Yalda and her daughter get settled in the United States. They found Yalda a place to live in Sacramento, California.

Yalda brings food home to her apartment in Sacramento.

After her arrival in the United States, Yalda faced many struggles and challenges. The apartment she and her daughter were placed in was rundown, dirty, and swarming with roaches and bedbugs. Crime was high in the neighborhood. And Yalda had little money because she had spent almost all her savings on the plane tickets to the United States.

THE STATES WHERE MOST PEOPLE RECEIVING SIVs HAVE RESETTLED

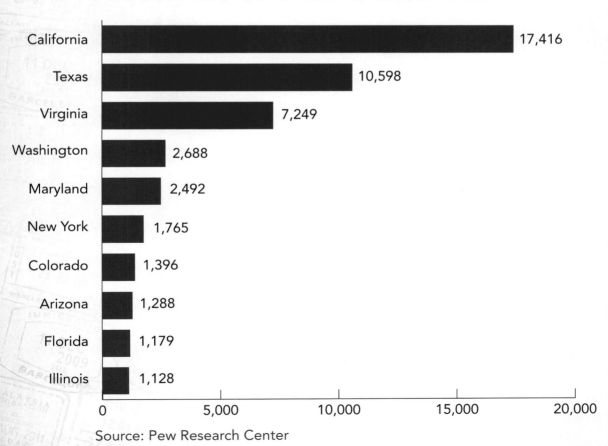

California	17,416
Texas	10,598
Virginia	7,249
Washington	2,688
Maryland	2,492
New York	1,765
Colorado	1,396
Arizona	1,288
Florida	1,179
Illinois	1,128

Source: Pew Research Center

However, Yalda was not alone. She found out that SIV immigrants can receive financial help and health care from the government for a few months. About a month later, Zabihullah's visa was approved, and he arrived in the United States. But neither of them had jobs, so they couldn't afford a car to get to Yalda's doctor's appointments. Instead they bought a bicycle, and Yalda learned how to ride it. Every week she had to bike 90 minutes each way to her doctor's office until her daughter Usna was born.

Soon Yalda came up with a plan to make a fresh start. She took special courses in childcare and earned a certificate that allowed her to work with children. Then she opened a small daycare business in her apartment so she could care for the children of other Afghani refugees. This allowed the mothers to attend school to learn English and enroll in job-training programs. Things were looking up for Yalda and her family.

Yalda runs a daycare business in her home.

WHAT'S NEXT?

More good news followed. Zabihullah got a job testing iPhones before they were sold to the public. But the job paid just $12 an hour, which was barely above **minimum wage**. Many other Afghani refugees also worked at the company.

Zabihullah's work schedule allowed Yalda to attend classes at a nearby college. The family's home daycare was just the first step toward building a new life in the United States. Yalda plans to continue her education and perhaps become a teacher or lawyer. She wants to help other newly arrived immigrants. "I want to work with people to help them," she said.

Yalda does homework for her college courses.

minimum wage—the lowest amount a company can legally pay a worker

Yalda and her husband, Zabihullah

Zabihullah also found time to help fellow Afghanis in Sacramento. Thousands of SIVs had accidentally left off the last names of the immigrants. Their first names were listed as their last names. The letters FNU, which stands for "first name unknown," were put on official documents. On every government document—school records, driver's licenses, medical reports—their first name was listed as FNU. This made finding a job and getting government services difficult. Zabihullah used his ability to write and speak English to file papers with the local courts for his neighbors. In all, he helped more than 100 people get their real names on documents.

Still, life in the United States has not been what Yalda expected. She and her family have struggled to make ends meet. Their tiny apartment is too small for a family of four, and it needs constant repair. The neighborhood is filled with violence, crime, and drugs. "My dream was a nice house, nice location," she said. "I worry about the children and what they see growing up here."

IN THE SCHOOLS

Many young Middle Eastern immigrants face numerous challenges attending school in the United States. Some children feel they are behind the American students, especially if they don't speak English well. Others are bullied because of **prejudice** against Middle Easterners. Many school districts in the United States offer special programs to help immigrant students learn to read, write, and speak English. Other programs are designed to encourage students to speak out against prejudice and discrimination.

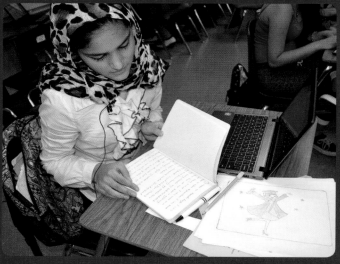

A young Afghani immigrant works on her English homework at a high school in California.

Even so, Yalda hopes for a successful future in America, little by little. Although she never drove in Afghanistan, Yalda learned to drive in Sacramento. "In Afghanistan it only costs a dollar or two for a taxi someplace, and they are everywhere," she said. "Here in the U.S., you need a car to get around." It's one small but important step toward making it in the United States.

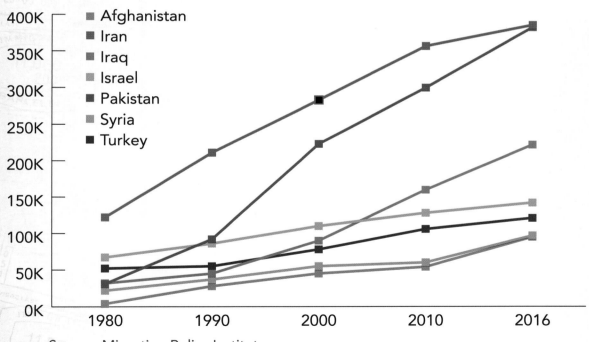

COUNTRIES OF BIRTH FOR U.S. IMMIGRANTS FROM THE MIDDLE EAST, 1980–2016

Legend:
- Afghanistan
- Iran
- Iraq
- Israel
- Pakistan
- Syria
- Turkey

Source: Migration Policy Institute

prejudice—hatred or dislike of people who belong to a certain social group, such as a race or religion

GLOSSARY

discrimination (dis-kri-muh-NAY-shuhn)—treating people unfairly because of their race, country of birth, or gender

executive order (ig-ZEK-yuh-tiv OR-dur)—an order that comes from the U.S. president or a government agency and must be obeyed like a law

expire (ik-SPIRE)—to reach the end of the time when something can be legally or properly used

immigrant (IM-uh-gruhnt)—someone who comes from one country to live permanently in another country

minimum wage (MIN-uh-muhm WAJE)—the lowest amount a company can legally pay a worker

passport (PAS-port)—an official booklet that proves a person is a citizen of a certain country; passports allow people to travel to foreign countries

persecution (pur-suh-KYOO-shuhn)—cruel and unfair treatment often because of race or religious beliefs

prejudice (PREJ-uh-diss)—hatred or dislike of people who belong to a certain social group, such as a race or religion

refugee (ref-yuh-JEE)—a person forced to flee his or her home country because of war, poverty, natural disaster, or persecution

translator (TRANZ-lay-tuhr)—someone who changes written or spoken material from one language into another

visa (VEE-zuh)—a government document that lets the holder enter and leave a foreign country and indicates how long he or she can stay there

READ MORE

Creager, Ellen. *Life as an Iraqi American.* One Nation for All: Immigrants in the United States. New York, PowerKids Press, 2018.

Glynne, Andy. *Ali's Story: A Real-Life Account of His Journey from Afghanistan.* Seeking Refuge. North Mankato, Minn.: Picture Window Books, 2018.

Mason, Helen. *A Refugee's Journey from Syria.* Leaving My Homeland. New York: Crabtree Publishing, 2017.

INTERNET SITES

Use FactHound to find Internet sites related to this book.

Visit www.facthound.com

Just type in 9781543513844 and go.

Check out projects, games and lots more at
www.capstonekids.com

CRITICAL THINKING QUESTIONS

1. Do you know where your family originally came from? Do you know why they came to America?

2. Study the infographic on page 29. Why do you think the number of immigrants from these countries has increased so much since 1990? Use evidence from the text to support your answers.

3. Imagine the children of Munther Alaskry and Yalda Kabiri are students in your class. What would you do to help them learn American customs? How could you learn about customs from their country?

INDEX

Alaskry, Munther, and family,
    10–14, 16, 18–19

challenges immigrants face, 23, 24,
    28

Detroit, Michigan, 6

ethnic groups
    Arabs, 4, 5, 6, 7
    Kurds, 4
    Persians, 4
    Turks, 4
executive order, 14, 16

Kabiri, Yalda, and family, 20–29

Middle East, 4, 5, 6, 7, 28
    Afghanistan, 6, 13, 20, 24, 26,
        27, 29
    Iraq, 6, 10, 12, 13, 14, 16, 18, 19
    Jordan, 10
    Lebanon, 6
    Qatar, 18
    Syria, 6, 9
    Turkey, 13, 14
    Yemen, 6

No One Left Behind, 19

Pilgrims, 6

reasons to immigrate, 6
    education, 6
    health care, 6
    jobs, 6
    natural disasters, 8
    poverty, 6, 8
    religious persecution, 6
    reuniting with family, 7
    war, 9
refugees, 8, 18, 24, 26
religious groups
    Christians, 4, 5, 6
    Jews, 4, 5, 9
    Muslims, 4, 5, 6

special immigrant visa (SIV), 12, 13,
    16, 19, 20, 23, 24, 27

terrorist groups
    al-Qaeda, 10, 12
    ISIS, 14
    Taliban, 20
Trump, Donald, 14, 16

U.S. military, 10, 12, 13, 19, 20

wars
    Iraq War, 10
    Syrian Civil War, 9
    War in Afghanistan, 20
waves of immigration, 9